LITTLE MIX

UNOFFICIAL

Publisher and Creative Director: Nick Wells
Project Editor: Polly Prior
Picture Research: Emma Chafer and Polly Prior
Art Director and Layout Design: Mike Spender
Layout Design: Jane Ashley
Digital Design and Production: Chris Herbert

Special thanks to: Laura Bulbeck, Emma Chafer, Esme Chapman and Daniela Nava

FLAME TREE PUBLISHING
Crabtree Hall, Crabtree Lane
Fulham, London SW6 6TY
United Kingdom
www.flametreepublishing.com

Website for this book: www.flametreepop.com

First published 2013

13 15 17 16 14
1 3 5 7 9 10 8 6 4 2

A CIP record for this book is available from the British Library upon request.

ISBN 978-0-85775-870-5

Printed in China

LITTLE MIX

Caroline Corcoran
Foreword by Alice Hudson

**FLAME TREE
PUBLISHING**

Contents

Foreword

Not since the 'Wannabe' heyday of The Spice Girls have I so believed in the ability of a Brit girl group. With catchy, energetic tunes and down-to-earth, sunny attitudes, Little Mix embody the nineties spirit of Girl Power I thought was dead and gone.

Jesy Nelson, Jade Thirlwall, Perrie Edwards and Leigh-Anne Pinnock each auditioned for *The X Factor* as soloists in 2011, but were deemed 'not quite ready' to make the cut as individuals. Lucky then, that judges – including mentor Tulisa Contostavlos – had the sense to put the four together. Little Mix went on to become the first-ever group to take the coveted *X Factor* crown, their harmonious renditions of hits like Beyoncé's 'If I Were A Boy' proving they were ready for anything. Since then, the girls have taken fame and pressure in their combined, unified stride and released a successful album, *DNA*.

In June 2013, it was even confirmed the Mixers had made their mark on the notoriously difficult US market, sales of *DNA* pushing it to No. 4 on the *Billboard* chart. This beats a record previously held by The Spice Girls' debut album *Spice* (1997) for the highest charting debut by a Brit all-female group.

When it comes to Little Mix, I have to agree with Baby Spice Emma Bunton. After being spotted dancing in her wellies and singing along to the Mixers at the 2013 Isle of Wight Festival, the now 37-year-old proclaimed, 'It's lovely to see the young ones flying the Girl Power flag.'

Go girls!

Alice Hudson

Against All Odds

It's probably the most unlikely success story since Bob the Builder got the Christmas No. 1. Little Mix were *never* going to win *The X Factor*. In fact, they were so unlikely to win *The X Factor* that during rehearsals for the first live show, paps shouted, 'See you on *This Morning* on Monday!' – a reference to the fact that the evicted acts did the rounds of morning TV shows following their exits.

How It All Began

In the green room, the odds were read out on the favourite to go. The verdict? The attractive girl band would be out in week one, of course; history had set a precedent, after all. But then a funny thing happened: Little Mix got through week one, then week two and soon they were hurtling towards the final. Jade, Jesy, Perrie and Leigh-Anne had broken the curse – both of the girl bands and of a group winning the show. Remember that not even the mighty One Direction had managed that.

'The girls are going to be the biggest girl band we've had for years. They're coming into the industry just at the right time when there's a big gap in the market for them.'

Tulisa on Little Mix

It hadn't been a simple road for the girls, though. Like One Direction before them, they were put together during the show, having never met each other beforehand. All four had had *something* in their auditions but not managed to wow the judges. Gary didn't like Jesy's version of 'Bust Your Windows', giving her a 'No' and telling her it was 'generic', while Tulisa, incredibly, told Perrie: 'I like you, but I'm not in love with you.'

Kelly Rowland felt differently, shouting, 'Your voice is crazy, yo!' after Perrie's performance of Alanis Morissette's 'You Oughta Know'.

When Leigh-Anne auditioned with Rihanna's 'Only Girl (In The World)', Kelly told her, 'I do see you in a girl band.' The seeds were sown and although the four girls got through to Boot Camp, their journeys as solo artists would end there.

'I used to be the shyest little thing ever. The thing that brought out my confidence is being in this group with these girls. Being around them has brought out the best in me. [If you struggle with feeling confident], my tip is to surround yourself with positive people and good friends.'

Leigh-Anne Pinnock

'We thought we were going to be voted off
The X Factor in the first week.'

Jesy Nelson

Boot Camp Brainwave

Instead, they were placed in two different groups: Jesy and Perrie in Faux Pas, alongside two other girls, and Jade and Leigh-Anne in a band called Orion. Neither group made it to Judges' Houses but then *The X Factor* bosses had a brainwave and the four girls were placed in a band together, performing under the name Rhythmix.

Later on Jade would give her verdict on why she thought the judges made that decision: 'I think they were watching us each week, observing who would get on,' she told the *Guardian*. 'But also, we were the same height and that's one of the things they said was really important.'

Thank god for genetics! A couple of teen growth spurts and the group as we know it may not exist today. Whatever the reason they were put together, though, it worked from the off. 'They look frickin' awesome together,' said Kelly Rowland the first time she saw the girls walk on stage as a unit.

During the live shows, their performance became the one you tuned in for. What would they do this week? The girls mixed it up, jumping from Nicki Minaj to ballads and mash-ups. They even managed to ride out a name change; it turned out that a Brighton charity were also called Rhythmix so the girls decided to take on a new moniker: Little Mix.

'My mum's boyfriend put a bet on us to win and ended up with £10,000 because the odds were so low on us winning!'

Jesy Nelson

Go, Girls!

In week seven Little Mix performed En Vogue's 'Don't Let Go', which became the turning point, perhaps, and the moment when the British public decided that, actually, maybe a girl band *could* win this – if a girl band were this good.

As they appeared on the Marks & Spencer Christmas advert, one fan tweeted after their victory was announced: 'Well its obvious little mix were gonna win, they were the ones at the end of the marks and spencer advert' [sic]. They weren't alone in that theory, especially considering the prominent vocals that the girls – in particular Perrie – were given on *The X Factor* charity single 'Wishing On A Star'; it was obvious that they were positioning themselves as winners.

Nonetheless, everyone was still surprised – none more so than the girls, perhaps – when in December 2011, after performances of Florence and The Machine's 'You've Got The Love', and a mash-up of 'Empire State Of Mind' and 'If I Ain't Got You' with mentor Tulisa, they actually did beat Amelia Lily and Marcus Collins to become the first ever group to take *The X Factor* crown.

'It means a lot because obviously we got a number one at Christmas with Cannonball, but that wasn't our song really, so now that we've become number one with our own song that we wrote, we're so proud, best feeling ever.'

Little Mix

Changing Their Life

Afterwards, critics were united in agreement that the right act won, with Stuart Heritage of the *Guardian* saying that they took the winning spot 'by spurning sexiness for accessibility'. However, he did balance that out with some criticism of the winners' song choice, adding that they won 'to a lesser extent, by making a tedious Damien Rice ballad sound marginally less unlistenable than their remaining rival Marcus Collins did'. Ouch.

Nevertheless, 'Cannonball' zoomed to the No. 1 spot, and Little Mix were free to move on to making music of their own choosing. Now signed to Simon Cowell's record label SYCO, and to Columbia in the US, the girls were squirrelled off into recording studios and our contact with them – except for the obligatory *The X Factor* tour – would be minimal until it was time for them to reveal the direction that they'd chosen now that the show's apron strings had been cut.

Pop Girl Power

Fast forward to 2013 and Little Mix have rocked up five Top 20 singles and a Top 3 album, and they have teamed up with some of the biggest names in the music industry. Perhaps it was an appetite thing; the Spice Girls were long gone, Girls Aloud were on a hiatus and at the time no-one was getting all that excited about The Saturdays – we were ready for a new wave of pop girl power.

And the girls are certainly happy with the nod to their perhaps most relevant predecessors. 'We were brought up listening to them,' says Perrie. 'So for people to say we are like the new version of the Spice Girls is just amazing, a massive compliment.'

In the Mix

Four girls who had never met, thrown together by fate … Well, fate *and* Gary Barlow, but that takes away some of the romanticism, so let's just go with fate. For Jade, this was third time lucky, as she turned up at *The X Factor* auditions in Birmingham in 2011 after having made it a far as Boot Camp in 2008 and 2010. It was her age (she was only 15 at her first audition) and her lack of confidence in herself that had stopped her going through, rather than her talent; self-confessed swot and head girl, Jade was an experienced singer already, performing at pubs and clubs in her local area with a good friend of hers: a certain Joe McElderry.

'When you go out looking like an absolute tramp and you see yourself the next day, you think: "Do you know what, it's five minutes in the morning putting a bit of mascara on and a bit of foundation and it saves a lot of flak."'

Perrie Edwards

'I describe my style as urban and street. I'm really influenced by the '80s and '90s, like The Fresh Prince Of Bel-Air. I wear lots of color. I also love Timberlands. Timberlands are my favorite thing in the world.'

Leigh-Anne Pinnock

It's In Their DNA?

Unbeknownst to Jade, of course, this was to be her year – but only because of some other girls who had turned up at the auditions around the country. In London, an Essex girl with big hair called Jessica, who had been to the Sylvia Young School and was currently working as a barmaid, had come along to try out. When she attempted to bail out in the queue, convinced she wouldn't get through, her mum Janis (everybody in their family has names beginning with 'J') persuaded her to stick around.

Elsewhere in the O2 queue was Leigh-Anne Pinnock, who had just passed her A levels and was working in Pizza Hut before she went to university. More used to performing Spice Girls routines with her sisters, Leigh-Anne was also having doubts, mostly because she was ill and sure she wouldn't perform at her best. Luckily they both stayed around.

Auditions For iPhones

At the other end of the country was a girl called Perrie Edwards. Named after a singer from rock band Journey, she had a musical heritage, as both her parents were singers. Although Perrie performed regularly at school, she always stood at the back because she thought she was 'just a normal singer'. This time, though, she was pushing herself to the front – but only because her mum had promised to get her an iPhone if she went along. Perrie headed to Glasgow with her mum, as the Newcastle auditions had been cancelled, but didn't tell anyone else that she was auditioning.

On the surface, the connections weren't clear but what Gary and the other judges obviously saw was a common thread, both in terms of a potential friendship and musically. The girls just gelled, fusing R&B, hip-hop and contemporary pop with amazing vocal harmonies; the music felt fresh and when the girls came to make videos, the same would be said for those.

'So sick of having to defend #PerrieEdwards in interviews. Who cares if she has the same hair as me I think she is adorable I <3 Little Mix!'

Kelly Osbourne on Twitter

'Jesy = Rocky/Urban/Street;

Jade = Geeky/Urban/Cute;

Leigh-Anne = Urban/Old School;

Perrie = Rocky/Hippy Boho.'

Little Mix on their style

Breath Of Fresh Air

Colourful, young and fun – exactly what an over-sexualized pop market had needed. 'I don't even have any sexy curves to show off — my chest is like flat pancakes,' said Perrie in an interview when the subject came up. 'We're only young as well. My mam would give us a slap if she saw me in my bra in a magazine.' How refreshing!

It was the same away from the music, as the girls seemed relatable and approachable; there was something there that was instantly appealing to teens: the crucial market with which girl bands on *The X Factor* had failed to connect before.

And they also had pretty good mentors: a certain *fairly* successful band called One Direction. 'They just said, "You have to enjoy what you do and you have to be confident,"' said Perrie, on the advice they'd received from the boys. '"You have to work your bum off and just go for it because it's a once in a lifetime opportunity. The day that you stop enjoying it is the day that it's going to get hard for you."'

Style Mix

The One Direction link certainly hasn't done them any harm, but another key part of Little Mix's brand is their styling. Whether it was deliberate or not, one thing that made these girls immediately different to other girl bands was that they were dancing and singing in trainers and jeans rather than thigh-baring leotards and killer heels. They also retained their own individualism: there was no matchy-matchy styling. Leigh-Anne sums it up perfectly: 'That's what I love about us, we all have our own look and can stand apart from the group but together it's a good mix.'

Perhaps, at a time when the world is looking at Rihanna taking her clothes off on Twitter for the fifteenth time that week and feeling rather bored, an important element of Little Mix's appeal is as something a bit more wholesome.

The girls have embraced their position as role models, giving confidence tips to teen magazines and extolling the virtues of individuality. 'If you want to wear something, all that matters is that *you* love it, not what other people think,' says Jesy. 'Learn to love yourself!'

'The nicest thing has been getting messages from girls who are being bullied, who say that now they don't feel alone.'

Jesy Nelson

Answering Back

The clothes are just emblematic, really; Little Mix have always stood for triumph over adversity: from being the winners in a show that habitually fails girl bands to Jesy's very public struggle with cyber bullies. In one performance on *The X Factor*, she actually broke down, as the online vitriol over her weight and appearance had got to her so much.

However, instead of breaking Jesy, it went on to become something she could help other young girls with. 'People are always commenting on how I look and it's because I'm a girl,' she told the *Sun*. 'You never see men's bodies being criticised in magazines.'

It was an important point and a win for feminism to see young female role models addressing this. 'Once I came off the TV show everyone thought I was on a strict diet but I'd just stopped going to the ITV canteen every day, with fry-ups every morning and chips for lunch, so I lost quite a bit of weight,' she said. 'I'm not going to suddenly become skinny — we're all different shapes and sizes in the band and people relate to us because we look normal … If I started to look like I'd lost two stone it would send out the wrong message.'

'People are always going to put you down. Whether you're in the media or not, you get bitchy people.'

Jesy Nelson

*'I like the idea that mums are watching us
and thinking we're good role models.'*
Jade Thirlwall

Hey, Girlfriend

And the 'message' is something that's crucial to Little Mix. Their videos show lots of girly bonding, and the lyrics have a strong female empowerment vibe. If there's ever any hostility then it's well hidden; what we see is a solid friendship and sisterhood. 'We are about being best friends, no bitchiness and good music,' Jade told the *Telegraph* in Australia.

The girls – or someone who works with them – have been savvy to their appeal and taken this girly connection with fans further. They brought out a range of nail wraps, promoted hair dye by getting out-there colour put on their own hair, took their promo missions directly to fans as they handed out ice-creams and hit social media in a big way. The girls tweet constantly and, crucially, make their relationship with fans feel like a two-way street.

'My style icon is Kelly Kapowski from Saved By The Bell. I also like Madonna's style when she was quite punk. I like Kelly's colourful style, especially for summer, but in the winter I try a bit of Madonna's style.'

Perrie Edwards

Perhaps it was even social media that provided the edge for them in the live *The X Factor* shows; their win was predicted after they showed the greatest growth in Twitter followers and Facebook fans. And when they *did* win, they built on this. New ideas such as 'Mixers Magnets' – an online competition to win a concert in your country – encourages fans to be active, part of a club. These ideas have created loyalty and a strong army of fans with their very own name; forget the Directioners: it's all about the Mixers.

'I think Little Mix have got a great future and I backed them ever since Judges' Houses pretty much.'

Olly Murs on Little Mix

Always Be Together

When 'Wings' was released – eight months after Little Mix won *The X Factor* – the reviewers were waiting with bated breath to see whether it was actually any good. Could the girls translate that to the charts?

Made To Fly

Music journalist Michael Cragg wrote: 'So why is "Wings" brilliant? Well, it's got everything you'd want to hear in a pop song in 2012. Horns! Big clomping beats! A gloomy dubstep bit! Double-time handclaps! Ridiculous vocal runs last heard on a Christina Aguilera single! A marching band that arrives out of nowhere! A slightly trite lyric about loving yourself no matter what! It's great …' OK, there are bits of critique in there but overall you can tell that he fancies a dance to it. And the other reviews had a similar vibe.

When the girls were asked if the song addressed bullies, they explained that it went wider than that. Jesy told the *Guardian* that it also referred to 'people telling you that you're not good enough. When I was at school and I told teachers I wanted to be a singer they'd say "Really? What's your backup plan? If you don't work hard you'll be at Tesco." This is a song about believing in yourself.'

'We just want to give off a positive message and positive vibes.'

Perrie Edwards

'We just feel like the luckiest girls in the world to be able to perform in front of 10,000 people at Wembley Arena.'

Jesy Nelson

Girl Band Feast

Then came the album. Check out the credits and you can tell that Cowell was taking no chances; there are writing credits for Nicola Roberts from Girls Aloud, Shaznay Lewis from All Saints and T-Boz from TLC on *DNA* (2012). If 'Wings' was a nice starter, this was a veritable girl band feast.

The album went to No. 3, an identical chart position to its namesake single. The girls told Tim Jonze at the *Guardian* that with 'DNA' the single 'if you strip it all back and get rid of all the scientific shenanigans then it's just a love song, really'.

Time For The Ballad

Third single 'Change Your Life' – the obligatory ballad – left fans and critics underwhelmed and charted only at No. 12, but there was no time to dwell: Little Mix had a tour to be getting on with. After zooming around the UK to 20 different venues, though, it was time for their next release, and this time things were about to take a seriously exciting turn, as the girls were to duet with none other than Missy Elliott.

'How Ya Doin' was released in the UK in April 2013 to huge expectation after the disappointing chart position of 'Change Your Life'. However, a controversial release date – the single came out midweek – was blamed for the fact that it peaked only at No. 16. The position also meant that the single received less airplay than it would have done otherwise, thus causing less buzz than a Missy collaboration seemed to warrant.

The girls stayed positive, though, and Jesy was especially excited about working with her idol. 'We honestly can't believe Missy is on our song!' she commented. 'She's been one of our biggest idols forever – it's incredible. As soon as we thought there might be a chance she'd appear on the track we did literally everything we could to make sure it happened.'

'How Ya Doin' served as the final single from *DNA* and the girls were back in the studio. And now? It was time for the 'difficult second album'.

'We're very approachable. We are four normal, silly, weird girls. We want people to feel like they can come up to us and have a chat. We're like your friends.'

Leigh-Anne Pinnock

'I asked the boys from One Direction how to make it in America. They basically said: "Be yourself and you can't go wrong. People know when you're trying to be someone you're not. Just be true to who you are."'

Leigh-Anne Pinnock

Little Mix: The Next Chapter

'We all have the same vision with how we want the next album to sound,' Jesy told *Digital Spy*, leaving every fan in the world thinking: 'Yes, but *what is it*?' – it's safe to say that anticipation is high. As well as being back in the studio, summer 2013 was also when Little Mix went on the road, with high-profile gigs at the likes of V and the Isle of Wight festivals.

Meanwhile, their profile was building in the US: as well as their album *DNA* going to No. 4 on the *Billboard* 200 (beating the Spice Girls' record for highest ever charting debut album by a girl group), they played on *Good Morning America* and had the cover of *Seventeen* magazine. Also, 'Wings' was featured on *Glee* and *American Idol*. Let's not play any of those things down: in the 'breaking America' game, they are seriously important moves.

'I think everyone's got different body shapes and sizes, and no-one's perfect, and I just think you have to love yourself for who you are. If everyone looked the same it would be boring.'

Jesy Nelson

And could a fly-on-the-wall TV show be on the cards too? 'We've always said we wanted to do it,' Perrie told Lorraine Kelly. 'It could be called A Little Bit Of Little Mix or something like that. We've always done video diaries for the fans, so this would be an extension of that.'

Further ahead than that may seem crazily forward thinking for girls with only one album behind them, but Little Mix have never been the types to aim low. So while there is no sign at all of them breaking up – 'We'll still be here with our zimmer frames,' says Perrie – they are already planning a Spice Girls-style reunion in 10 years' time. The girls' ambition can perhaps be summed up in this quote from Jesy to the Australian press when Little Mix were out there: 'We just want to take over the world … We want to be everywhere, literally everywhere.'

And with ambition like that, you wouldn't bet against them.

'We've all got a good ear for sound and music.
And we practise over and over, then we record
it on our phones so that when we go to
sleep we can listen to it in bed.'

Perrie Edwards

Little Mix Vital Info

Perrie
Birth Name   Perrie Louise Edwards
Birth Date   10 July 1993
Birth Place   South Shields, Tyne and Wear, England
Nationality   British
Height   162 cm (5 ft 3 in)

Leigh-Anne
Birth Name   Leigh-Anne Pinnock
Birth Date   4 October 1991
Birth Place   High Wycombe, Buckinghamshire, England
Nationality   British
Height   162 cm (5 ft 3 in)

Jesy
Birth Name   Jessica Louise 'Jesy' Nelson
Birth Date   14 June 1991
Birth Place   Romford, Essex, England
Nationality   British
Height   162 cm (5 ft 3 in

Jade
Birth Name   Jade Amelia Thirlwall
Birth Date   26 December 1992
Birth Place   South Shields, Tyne and Wear, England
Nationality   British
Height   162 cm (5 ft 3 in)

Online

little-mix.com/gb/home: Official website of Little Mix, with all the latest band news and photos

twitter.com/LittleMixOffic: Follow @LittleMixOffic and see what the girls and other Mixers are talking about!

facebook.com/LittleMixOfficial: Find out all the latest Little Mix news, with posts, music videos and events

newlook.com: Head here to buy Little Mix's official false nail collection, including wraps in a variety of patterns!

flametreepop.com: Celebrity, fashion and pop news, with loads of links, downloads and free stuff!

Acknowledgements

Caroline Corcoran (Author)
Caroline Corcoran is a freelance writer and editor who has previously worked at *3am Online*, *More!*, *Sugar*, *Fabulous* and *Heat*. She now writes for a variety of publications and websites on celebrity, TV, popular culture, any issues that are relevant to women and most things that people are gossiping about on Twitter. She is also writing her first novel. Follow her on Twitter @cgcorcoran.

Alice Hudson (Foreword)
From New Zealand, Alice fused twin passions for writing and music while a student, reviewing and interviewing international bands and DJs. She is currently based in London, writing and researching for corporate clients across a wide range of sectors, from health and fitness and financial services, to social media and entertainment.

Picture Credits
All images © **Getty Images**: FilmMagic: 11, 24; Getty Images Entertainment: 8, 12, 15, 16 & back cover, 18, 23, 26, 28, 35, 43, 44; Getty Images for Extra: 7; Redferns via Getty Images: 21; WireImage: 1, front cover & 3 & 46, 31, 32, 36, 39, 40.